Fingertip Devotions

Amy Bolding

BAKER BOOK HOUSE
Grand Rapids, Michigan 49506

Paperback edition issued 1982

ISBN: 0-8010-0798-4

Second printing, May 1983

PHOTOLITHOPRINTED BY CUSHING - MALLOY, INC.
ANN ARBOR, MICHIGAN, UNITED STATES OF AMERICA

Dedicated to Jane, a nurse
who loves her patients.

WORDS OF APPRECIATION:

In this book you will find a number of poems written by Edward V. Wood. Mr. Wood runs a very successful business in Dallas, Texas.

One Christmas I was visiting a Nursing Home near Dallas. The woman I was visiting showed me a poem on a small card. The poem had been in a basket of fruit she received. I liked the poem so much I wrote the author and asked permission to put it in one of my books.

He sent me a nice package of his poems with a letter saying I could use them. I am very grateful to Mr. Wood.

Some of the poems are written by a girlhood friend, Jewel Alice McLeod. I had lost track of her for a number of years and happened to find one of her poems in a magazine. We started corresponding and she sent me poems and permission to use them.

One very lovely poem was written by my only son, James T. Bolding, Jr. I am indebted to him for all the encouragement he has given me as I try to write.

Other poems are written by my husband who is very patient and kind to take time out of a busy work schedule to write for my devotions.

My books would be so dull without the love and help of others. I would like to say, thank you.

Amy Bolding

CONTENTS

1

Your Talents

"And Barak said unto her, If thou wilt go with me, then I will go: but if thou wilt not go with me, then I will not go. And she said, I will surely go with thee: . . . And Deborah arose, and went with Barak to Kedesh."
—Judges 4:8, 9

The children of Israel were in great need of a military leader. Barak had no talent for leadership, yet he knew how to fight a battle. He went to a woman, Deborah, a prophetess, and asked her for help and advice. She went with him and he was not afraid to lead the Children of Israel to success in battle.

Deborah was a leader and not afraid to use her talents. She turned her gift over to God and became one of the greatest Judges of Israel.

The Bible is filled with stories of people who turned their talents over to God and were led to victory and success.

David had only a sling shot at a time when he might have felt the need for an army. He was offered someone else's sword but he preferred his own weapon and God's blessing. He was able to kill the giant by using his own sling shot.

We do not all have the same talents, but we do all have some talents. The question is will we make the most of what we have by asking God to take charge and direct us?

How well I remember the time I turned my talent over to God! I had written a number of articles for religious magazines and sold them. My heart was really set on being a leader in some organization, not sitting quietly at home and writing. God awakened me by striking a blow at my health. I realized I had to stop going from place to place and meeting to meeting.

Sitting at the breakfast table after my husband had gone to work, I put my head on my arms and turned my problems and my talents, if I had any, over to God.

After that period of prayer I arose and went to the hallway where there was a bookcase. Taking a book at random I glanced through it, "You can write a better book than that," something seemed to say. I started that day. God seemed to lead all the way. My first book was accepted the first time I sent it to a publisher – not because I had so much talent, but because God had a need for that little bit and turned it into good for His glory.

Whatever your talent, dedicate it to God and He will lead you to the place to use it. When God comes in all His power and glory we will render an account of what we have done with the talents He has entrusted to us.

A talent is the ability to do a certain thing, perhaps a little better than the average person. It is a trust we are to take seriously. It is not so important what your talent is, as what you do with it.

The smallest talent turned over to God can be an instrument for good in His service.

Joshua had a gift of generalship; Jacob had the ability to make money; Moses had a rod; Miriam had a musical talent. Each used his talents in service.

Isn't it wonderful that we do not all have the same gifts? If we take our gifts and wrap them in a napkin they may not wear out but they certainly will do no good and will not develop into greater gifts.

MAN'S EXTREMITY IS GOD'S OPPORTUNITY

I prayed a sincere prayer – I thought –
That God's will for me be wrought.
  Earnesly I prayed – I'll have you know!
  "Lord, lead where you'll have me go."

No doubt the Lord gave every sign,
Pointing the path that should be mine.
  Instead of seeing the way He led,
  To my own course turned I, instead;

Until at last, through trials sore,
Of my own way I'd have no more.
  Then weary, broken and in pain,
  Once more – in need – to Him I came.

"Lord, teach me how to heed Thy will –
How to listen and be still.
  Teach me to rightly read the signs –
  How to know Thy will from mine."

– Edward V. Wood

2

Leave Some Things Behind
(New Year)

Brethren, I count not myself to have apprehended: but this one thing I do, forgetting those things which are behind, and reaching forth unto those things which are before." – Philippians 3:13

Growing up in a minister's home, I was often forced to move from town to town. How I hated to leave my friends! Often we would move on a borrowed truck belonging to some church member and we would have to leave some of our half-worn-out toys or favorite junk behind. How I detested moving day and the pain it brought.

After I was grown, with children of my own, we were moving from East Texas to West Texas. The new church sent a spacious commercial van to move our belongings. When all was loaded my youngest daughter noticed her doll buggy had been left out. With a look of determination on her usually sweet face she took the worn-out toy to the moving man and said, "You are not going to leave this out."

We come to face a new year and many of us look about at our pet peeves and faults and say, "I'll not leave you behind."

Yet we must leave some things behind if we are to have a happy year.

First, let us forget our past sins. They are in the past and

God has promised to forgive us and blot them out if we are His children. At times we have all caused disappointments to those we love because of our shortcomings. Forget the past, reach forth for better things.

Second, let us forget any extraordinary accomplishments we may have had in the past and determine to reach for new heights in this new year. Achieve new successes. God has blessed each of us with some fortunate things. We are not to be conceited but to press on to new and better things.

Third, we should forget our failures of the past year. Why take the pain, grief and sorrow into a new year. Life always has some storms, some losses; but we need not take the memory of them into the new year. We must accept our sorrows and failures as part of life's journey and press on to new achievements.

Fourth, we should leave behind in the old year all our bad habits. New Year's Day is a wonderful time to make a fresh start and determine to break the detrimental habits we have accumulated.

Moving into a new year, or a new home or town, does not require leaving everything behind. There are many things we should plan to take with us.

What can we take into the new year? We do not want to be like my little daughter, who at the last moment could not stand to see the doll buggy left behind. We want to plan what we shall take into the coming months.

First, we want to take love for others. We want success this year but not at the expense of others. We must take love if we are to be happy and have lasting joy.

Second, we must take with us gratitude to God for His many blessings to us; gratitude to our friends for their patience with our shortcomings; gratitude for life and health as God has given to us in the past; and gratitude for an opportunity to start a new year with its promise of good things to come.

Third, along with gratitude, we must always take appreciation. Let us show our appreciation more in the future. We must appreciate our mothers and fathers, our relatives and friends. People have often been kind to us in the years past; so we want to take appreciation for kindness shown us.

Fourth, we want to take the chip off our shoulder and kindle a fire of love with it for those we meet. Think kindly of all you meet. Seek the welfare even of those to whom you cannot give your friendship.

Fifth, we will need a lot of truth and justice as we begin our journey – justice for others and truth in our own hearts.

Sixth, we must always take plans for service, to God and to others.

Seventh, we want to take the peace in our hearts God promised to those who would serve Him. The world is in a state of unrest and turmoil but the Christian can go along serenely and calmly knowing who is walking with him into the unknown of a new period in his life.

JOURNEY

As I begin my pilgrimage
  Into this brand-new year,
What shall I take along with me
  That I some heart may cheer?

Not greed for gain, nor doubts, nor fears,
  Not vanity, nor pride;
Not grudges, guarrels, hate nor tears,
  But love and peace to guide.

I shall delight to take the Lord
  Throughout each day with me
And try to share His wondrous love
  With everyone I see.

I'll share the joy Christ gives to me,
  And face life with a smile;
I'll try my best like Him to be,
  And serve for Him each mile.

– J. T. Bolding

3

Harvest Time

"For thus saith the Lord of hosts, the God of Israel; The daughter of Babylon is like a threshingfloor, it is time to thresh her: yet a little while, and the time of her harvest shall come." – Jeremiah 51:33

"The harvest is passed, the summer is ended, and we are not saved." – Jeremiah 8:20

In nature everything moves toward a common harvest time. Summer leads to autumn, the season of the year when fruit is ripe, and nuts, corn, cotton are ready to harvest.

In life youth moves toward middle age and middle age moves toward old age. As life progresses it becomes richer and fuller with the fruits of living. Some are good fruits and some are bad, but all will be gathered in a harvest of some kind.

Time is like a threshing floor to which every person must bring his life to be tried. We all go forth to sow. Some of us will come to harvest time earlier than others, but all will eventually face the harvest. We cannot go back over the years to replant as farmers do. We have only one chance to sow – today.

Nature can increase the size of a fruit but it cannot change the kind. We have hearts filled with wrong things at times, but God who is ruler of all nature can change our lives. He can help us to sow good fruit and reap a good harvest.

Lincoln once closed an address by saying: "I have said nothing but what I would be willing to live by and, if it be the pleasure of Almighty God, to die by."

Most great men have great ideals and sow the seed to reap a harvest of success. We have all heard the slogan, "Think Big."

How can we do less than sow big? Sow for a harvest we will reap throughout all eternity.

In the days of slavery a prominent plantation owner died. His friends came from far and near to attend the funeral services. One man from out of town said to one of the grief-stricken slaves: "I hope your master has gone to heaven."

"I's afraid he has not gone there," replied the faithful slave. "I never heard him speak of that place."

"Maybe he just didn't mention it," the man said.

"When he go to New Orleans he always get ready fo' two or three weeks. I never see or hear him getting ready fo' no place called heaven."

Whether we get ready for a harvest time or ignore it, the time will come when the wheat will be separated from the chaff of life.

We recently drove through the wheat belt. Wheat fields were almost ready for the combines. Men were tinkering with them, getting them in perfect running order before starting the harvest.

To youth all roads seem open. There is school and a choice of careers. As one grows older the harvest of life grows nearer and the fields of opportunity become fewer. A man of sixty does not like to start on a fresh career or way of life. So at whatever stage of life we find ourselves, a harvest may be very near, and we want to be ready.

Some people are going to reap a happier harvest than others because they are working instead of weaping over their lot in life. Some will be happier because they boost others instead of knocking them.

Harvest Time

Romans 14:12 tells us, "... every one of us shall give account of himself to God."

We do not have to answer for the tares sown by other people. We must reap our own individual harvest just the way we sowed it throughout the years of our lives.

A mother took her children to the seed counter at the store and let each child pick a package of seed to plant. The little girl quickly selected a package of flower seed because the picture on the package was so pretty. The boy liked corn on the cob so he selected a package of corn seed. At harvest-time the little girl was bitterly disappointed because she had no corn. Her pretty flowers had bloomed and faded away.

Many people who choose to plant for pleasure and gaudy looks will be disappointed when the harvest of life comes.

GOD HAS A PLAN

Are you aimlessly wandering down life's road
With no destination in view?
Are you restless and weary in life's abode?
The Saviour is calling for you!

When Daniel was captured and taken away
To a land unknown to his soul,
He was tempted and tried by night and by day,
Yet he gave his Lord full control!

When you earnestly take Him into your heart,
When nothing from Him you withhold,
You will find that from you He will ne'er depart
He will hear and will save your soul!

God has a plan for your life,
He's tenderly calling today!
Believe and accept the Saviour divine
And He will show you the way!

– Jewel Alice McLeod

4

The Wine of Life

"My days are swifter than a weaver's shuttle, and are spent without hope." – Job 7:6

"The thief cometh not, but for to steal, and to kill, and to destroy: I am come that they might have it more abundantly." – John 10:10

On a very hot afternoon my youngest grandchild asked for a drink of water. I gave her a glass full but when it was finished she said, "More please."

Life may be filled with successes or failures, but at the close with sadness we write across the last day, "Too short." Job, although suffering from many earthly troubles, said, "My days are swifter than a weaver's shuttle." He also said, "My days are swifter than a post: they flee away" (9:25).

From time to time all of us have said, "Life is too short for me to accomplish all the things I want to do."

Since the wine of life soon runs out of the cup and we are here no more, we must choose wisely what we will do with the day allotted us.

Jesus knowing His allotted time would be very short, but also knowing He had a mission, said, "I am come that they might have it [life] more abundantly."

Someone has said, "Man's life is so short he has time to gather only one golden bough; passing on, he leaves whole forests behind."

The Wine of Life

A small girl was told she could buy something for her birthday in the variety store. Giving her a dollar, the mother put her inside the door and went to wait in the car. After a long, long time the child came back. Putting her packages on the car seat, she burst out crying.

"What is wrong dear? I thought you would be happy with a whole dollar to spend!" the mother said.

"I am happy with what I bought, but I am crying because I had to leave so much behind in the store."

Many a youth flits through school days – neglecting to study, and living only for fun. Then one day he must leave childhood behind, but he is not prepared for the adult world. He grasped only the bough of fun and left the forest of learning behind.

"Mother, may I go back and get more?" the crying child asked.

"No, dear, you have spent your money and there will not be any more for a long time."

Life only promises us today. We may spend it well or we may waste it. It is our life, but how we spend it determines our destiny.

The privileges to study, to grow, to witness, and even to live, comes from God. We are expected to make the very most of our days as they pass. Life is a trust and we are to make the most of it.

Ruth made a great decision when she turned away from her native land and went with Naomi.

Noah could easily have refused to preach, to build the ark, to enter the ark when it was built, but he chose to obey God.

Nehemiah was a cupbearer for a king, yet he found a way to make his life useful and worthwhile for his own people.

Abraham could have turned his back on Lot, but he wanted to help his nephew. He lived a life for others, yet God blessed him greatly.

One of the sad stories in the Bible is about the ten spies who refused to believe they could conquer the land God had promised. They, too, had to leave the forest behind.

The rich young ruler had opportunity to grasp life eternal, but because of the love of money he turned away.

Many of us know people who have wasted their lives because someone hurt their feelings. A small quarrel in a family may grow until it splits the family.

How are you spending your life?

STOP AND THINK!

If in boldness you do venture
From the pathway of the herd –
If above the routine level
You seek flight – like soaring bird –
If beyond the common market,
With its tumult and its din,
You would climb upon the mountain,
Why should folks call that a sin?

If you leave the dusty pathway
That the masses long have trod –
If you count your many blessings,
And give praise and thanks to God
That He's given you the courage
To stand upon your feet –
Just why should the willy-nilly
So let out a plaintive bleat?

Let them say you are "demanding" –
As the race of life you run –
That you're "odd" – a kind of "rover" –
Demanding place in the "sun."
So have all who've gone before you
Been so classed by thinkers small –
Who can only slur and slander
All of those who stand up tall.

– Edward V. Wood

5

Ways to Honor Mothers
(Mother's Day)

"Honor thy father and thy mother, as the Lord thy God hath commanded thee; that thy days may be prolonged, and that it may go well with thee, in the land which the Lord thy God giveth thee."

– Deuteronomy 5:16

You owe your mother thanks for the best part of your education. Who taught you to speak the first words you know? Who taught you to hold a spoon and feed yourself? Who cared for you when you were the most helpless of all creatures, a tiny baby? Who gave you life at great cost in suffering and pain?

Someone once said to a very successful man," I congratulate your mother for having such a son."

"Oh, no," the great man quickly replied, "Congratulate me, the son, for having such a mother."

It is an inborn nature for us to love and honor our mothers. Mothers form the first and best ideals in the minds of children. A mother who was proud of several accomplished children was asked how she had managed to instill in them the desire to be great.

"Early in childhood I taught them a little verse by quoting

it to them often," she replied, "That verse stood by them as they progressed through life."

The mother's poem:

> "When things go wrong as they sometimes will,
> When the road you're trudging seems all up hill,
> When the funds are low and the debts are high,
> And you want to smile, but you have to sigh,
> When care is pressing you down a bit,
> Rest, if you must – but don't you quit!"

Mothers are great for getting young folks started. Even in old age most of us would rather please our mothers than anyone else.

We are commanded in the Scriptures to honor our mothers. How can we best honor them? All cannot be famous; all cannot be great in a financial way; all are not born to be great leaders; yet all can honor their parents.

One of the best ways, at all ages, to honor your mother is to do your best in self-improvement. Keep trying to reach your potential. When I was young, mothers frequently said to their daughters as they began to think seriously about marriage, "You make your bed and you must lie on it."

Many a girl thought twice before marrying because her mother had instilled in her the fact that marriage was permanent and what we choose remains with us.

Another way to honor mothers is to love them. A mother loves her child, not because he is pretty or good or smart but because he is hers – bone of her bone and flesh of her flesh.

A wonderful way to honor a mother is to be frugal and careful with clothes, money, and possessions. Some mothers find it necessary to work so that their children may have a roof over their heads and clothes to wear. It is a sacrifice for mothers to leave the home and work. Children should do their share by being conservative and careful.

The greatest way we can honor our mothers is by loving

God and serving Him. A Christian mother thinks first about the spiritual welfare of her children.

We can also honor our mothers by being chaste. How proud we are when we feel our children are virtuous, pure, and modest.

Parents are honored when their children are pure in design and expression. One does not have to be rich to be refined, nor does one have to be poor to be vulgar. It is a matter of the heart and the training.

Mother is a magic word, making us think of home and familiar places that have become dear to us. God mentions mothers often in the Bible. Some were good and some were bad, but all deserved respect from their children because they gave them life.

The promise we all want to claim is the promise of long life upon the earth. God made that promise to those who honor their parents.

One day I was visiting in a nursing home. I was in a room occupied by two women, both bed patients. The son of one came in and went immediately to his mother and kissed her. Then he placed a chair near the bed and took her paralyzed hand in his and held it. He told her how well she was looking and how pretty her gown was. She tried in her feeble way to smile and acknowledge his presence.

In a few moments a man and his wife came in. The lady in the other bed was this man's mother. He stood barely inside the door, made no attempt to speak to his mother or even to look at her if he could help it. His wife went to the bed and asked how she was feeling and if she needed anything. In a moment they were gone. All in the room could see that it had been merely a duty call and not a call of love and devotion.

Mothers do not ask for expensive gifts, nor even too much time; but oh, how they long for a little show of love and affection.

Another mother I know saves all the mail she gets from

her children. She reads it over and over when she is lonely. She knows each child's problem and often as she reads she asks God's blessings on her children.

MY DEAR MOMS

Each day, each hour, her love she's shown,
Each year to me she's dearer grown;
Each prayer at eve is for her own –
My dear Moms!

Her cheer affords such joy and peace,
Her care provides my life new lease,
Her love I know will never cease –
My dear Moms!

My thoughts are never from her denied,
My hopes, my joys with her abide,
My fears and cares are at her side –
My dear Moms!

Dear Lord, watch o'er her day by day,
May she have a happy way,
Shower her life with love's sweet ray –
My dear Moms!

– Jewel Alice McLeod

6

Opportunity
(Young People)

"And he dreamed, and behold a ladder set up on the earth, and the top of it reached to heaven: and behold the angels of God ascending and descending on it."
—Genesis 28:12

In the dream described in the above scripture, Jacob had an opportunity to make a covenant with God. We might say he had a ladder of opportunity. God renewed to Jacob the promises He had made many years before to his grandfather Abraham and to his father Isaac.

John Flavel, English clergyman of the 1600's, wrote, "Opportunities are golden spots of time. Like the pearl in the shell of the oyster, they are of much more value than the shell that contains them. There is much time in a short opportunity."

Life is so short we must make the most of each opportunity lest it pass quickly by and be lost.

A small boy was watching the gutter after a rain storm to see what treasure he could pluck from the water rushing by. He was so busy watching a small piece of wood as it tumbled about that he failed to see a limp, crumpled dollar bill. His small sister caught it and was very elated that she had won such a prize.

Often in life we miss opportunities because we are too

busy looking at some useless pleasure or worthless pastime. Youth must make the most of opportunities for education and mental development, for they pass quickly with the years.

Many times we miss great opportunities for wealth because we are like the miner who was looking for gold. Waiting to find the nuggets, he let the tiny grains of gold pass by.

Most people find they must save a little each month in order to have some security for few find great wealth suddenly.

The first step toward seizing opportunities is to decide what kind of opportunity one will seek.

Seeking to lay the foundation for a godly character is to be desired. Looking for greater ways to accomplish good is also desirable.

I know a red-headed city boy who was determined to be a farmer. The farm to him looked far away and hard to get. He worked hard after college and saved every penny toward the farm of his dreams, but farms were very expensive and money hard to save. Then one night someone introduced him to the only daughter of a prosperous farmer. He fell in love with her (or the father's farm) immediately. He told her of his dream and in a few months they were married. Her father, a very wise and shrewd man, helped the son-in-law start paying for his dream farm. Well, at least he had kept himself open and ready for the opportunity to own a farm when it came.

In contrast, another boy, son of divorced parents, wanted a college education. His father was helping him go to school. In his sophomore year he started dating a beautiful blond girl. His father and his mother both advised him against getting involved until he finished school. He refused to stop keeping company with the girl. Her morals and her heart were not nearly as pretty as her face. Soon the boy was forced to marry her. His father washed his hands of him. He had to leave school and start to work. In two years time the girl left him, in deep debt and with a shattered life. He wasted his opportunity for the desire of his heart, an education.

Many people do not waste their opportunities by meeting the wrong companions or making the wrong choices. They simply dream away their chances by sitting and building air-castles when they should be working. We must be active and firm in making choices which will lead to our goals.

A wealthy young woman was very proud of a string of real pearls her mother had given her. They were worth a great amount of money and she had been warned to keep them in a safe. However, she liked to wear them constantly. One day as she walked by the sea shore she decided to take a little boat ride. The sun was warm and she lay back in the boat to doze a moment. One hand was on her pearls. As she slept the hand moved and the string was broken, one by one the pearls slipped off and were lost forever.

As we slumber, unaware of our golden opportunities, they slip away one by one and are lost forever.

TAKE CARE, MY SON

Take care, my son, your life to plan
  As you would build a castle strong;
With close attention to the man
  You now are building while you're young.

A castle built on lofty ground
  Does there its loveliness retain
In pictured strength for all around
  To see and long its heights to gain.

And so 'tis true with lofty aim –
  With spires stretched out to meet its God
The noble soul bears noble name
  That will not lie beneath the sod.

And yet who builds yon castle strong,
  So solid laid on granite base,
Builds not that he may please the throng,
  But there to have a better place.

Heed not the taunts of base and low,
 Who ne'er can rise to lofty heights –
Who on their downward way will go
 While you will rise in noble flight.

The soul that sets its gaze on high
 And yearns for time to set it free
Will find its means for higher flight,
 And thus will greater glory see.

Take care, my son, your life to plan
 As you would build a castle strong;
With close attention to the man
 You now are building while you're young.

– Edward V. Wood

7

Divide Your Sunshine

"For the Lord God is a sun and shield: the Lord will give grace and glory: no good thing will he withhold from them that walk uprightly." – Psalm 84:11

One cold Sunday morning I rang for the elevator in our church.

When the door opened I stepped in and spoke to the man running the elevator.

"Sure is cold in here." I shivered. "You never will get any sunshine running this elevator."

"Well, now you are wrong. You brought in a nice big ray of sunshine when you stepped in."

I felt ashamed, for I had spoken out of habit. The elevator operator had been lonely for someone to speak and show an interest in him. After all, he was not paid to run the elevator, it was just a labor of love.

We are to share our sunshine with others if we would make our corner of the world brighter.

Once I knew a young woman everyone called "Sunshine." No one seemed to know what her real name was. There was no doubt about why she was called Sunshine. She was always the first at a neighbor's home when there was need. She never failed to have an encouraging word for others in their problems or projects. Besides just being a ray of sunshine away from home, she shared her home with an invalid father-in-law.

Each person has some sunshine in his life. Yet not all people share their sunshine with others.

A lady we had been trying to get as a member of our Sunday School class bluntly said: "I don't want to get involved. I am tender hearted and if I go to Sunday School and hear of a need I give too much."

So she prefers to live isolated and without friends, rather than to divide her sunshine with others.

A beautiful song goes like this:

> Walking in sunlight all of my journey,
> Over the mountains, thro' the deep vale,
> Jesus has said, "I'll never forsake thee,"
> Promise divine that never can fail.
>
> Heavenly sunlight, heavenly sunlight,
> Flooding my soul with glory divine.
> Hallelujah, I am rejoicing, singing His praises,
> Jesus is mine.

It does, at times, cost to divide sunshine; but didn't Christ commission us to love others? What is love except the sharing of the sunshine in our own lives?

A little girl came in from a morning away from home.

"What have you been doing?" her mother asked.

"Oh I have been happying up Mrs. Brown's little baby."

"How do you happy up a baby?" the curious mother asked.

"Just give it a little shake and lots of love talk."

So a little girl was happy because she had made a small baby happy. The baby's mother was happy to have a few moments to work quietly. The father came home to a well-cooked meal and a tidy house – all because one little girl shared her sunshine.

The more we try to make others happy, the happier we shall be ourselves.

Divide Your Sunshine

Have you ever thought about the fact that you may be entrusted with the only ray of sunshine some person will see and feel all day? What if you hide that ray of sunshine under a frown!

The sunshine of happiness is something that must be shared with others. When we keep our joys without sharing them they lose some of their flavor.

Last night our phone rang rather late. A friend was calling, all excited and happy. She had just received a call from an unwed mother's home and been told she could come and pick up a new baby. She had to share her joy with others.

Have you ever noticed how much fun children have with tea parties? They always want others to drink their make-believe tea.

Romans 12:10 reads, "Be ye kindly affectioned one to another."

An old adage goes: "To do a kind deed, wherever we can, is good for bird and beast and man."

Each person has a bit of sunshine in his hand. Christians have a particlar kind of sunshine to share with their neighbors.

We want our lives to be beautiful, powerful, fruitful. If God's love is our constant companion, we will be able to spread sunshine. There are a few rules we might follow if we would spread and divide our sunshine:

First, we must make the most of ourselves. Use all the opportunities we have for self-improvement.

Second, we must set a good example, for others see the way we look and act.

Third, we must be ever ready to console the sad and downhearted.

Fourth, we must remember we cannot divide what we do not have; so we must first fill our lives with the sunshine of God's love.

Fifth, we must learn to be content with our lot in life.

Seriously speaking:

A laugh is just like sunshine.
It freshens all the day,
It tips the peak of life with light,
And drives the clouds away.
The soul grows glad that hears it
And feels its courage strong.
A laugh is just like sunshine
For cheering folks along.

A laugh is just like music.
It lingers in the heart,
And where its melody is heard
The ills of life depart;
And happy thoughts are crowding
Its joyful notes to greet;
A laugh is just like music
For making living sweet.

— Selected

8

Be Somebody

"Pilate therefore said unto him, Art thou a king then? Jesus answered, Thou sayest that I am a king. To this end was I born, and for this cause came I into the world, that I should bear witness unto the truth. Every one that is of the truth heareth my voice." – John 18:37

"The earth is the Lord's and the fulness thereof; the world, and they that dwell therein" (Ps. 24:1).

We should all be filled with gratitude for the life God has given us. God did not allow us to come into the world without a purpose or cause for our being alive.

Millions today seem to be searching for life in its fullest joy and glory. We can find that joy and peace by being grateful to God and by being of service in Christ's kingdom.

We are not God, yet we were created by Him – and He has a specific purpose for each of us.

A young man was fed up with life. He could not seem to find the place he was made to fit. He decided he would take his own life and end his misery. He took a bottle of carbolic acid to his room and swallowed it. As he lay suffering, he saw the world in greater clarity than ever before. His mouth and throat were on fire; his stomach was in such pain he screamed in agony. Suddenly he realized he had not really tried to be somebody. He wanted to live and try again.

Wanting to live was not enough and he lost his life in a few hours. He realized too late the precious gift of life and its importance to each of us.

It is natural for each of us to want to be somebody. It gives life significance. Women want their homes to express their personalities; men want to advance in their work. Yet no one of us can be happy just to to be somebody for his own selfish interest, for self-centeredness never makes people truly happy.

Each of us must want to be what Christ wants us to be if we are to be happy. To be somebody merely to exercise power over others will not bring happiness. We must place ourselves in God's power, in His will; then we will reflect His glory.

My husband and I were stopped by a beggar as we walked from a convention meeting to our hotel. I was quite frightened, but after we had given the man some money he said, "I was not afraid to ask you because I saw your badge and knew you were from the church meeting."

For him we were somebodies because we were there attending a church convention.

We are not to be somebodies with a lot of false pride. We are to worship in humility; pride should take a back seat. We are to show to the world where we stand and what we want to be by the way we act and live.

Many years ago when people were not afraid to allow strangers to spend the night with them, a traveler came to a farm house just at dusk. He asked to spend the night and the farmer said he could. The farm family were not religious and never attended church. When it was time for bed the visitor seemed to hesitate.

"Do you need something else?" the farm wife asked.

"Well, I always read the Bible and have a prayer before I retire. Would your family like to join me?"

The woman was embarrassed, for she had no idea what

family devotions involved. "If you will do all the reading and praying," she answered.

So the stranger took from his bag a well-worn Bible and read. Then he prayed for the family and asked God to bless them.

All went to bed and slept soundly because they knew a stranger who was so close to God could bring only good to their home. He was somebody because he was not afraid to show his belief in God.

Be somebody in making decisions. It is said of Jesus, "He spoke as one having authority."

A friend of mine said he lost great sums of money because whenever he was confronted with an opportunity he was afraid to make a decision.

Parents and teachers become somebodies to children when they speak with authority.

Be somebody on the journey of life. Whom will you follow as you take that journey! Will you see needs and try to right wrongs? Will you follow the good or the bad element in your community?

Be somebody in forgiveness. Be big enough to forgive those who mistreat you. Jesus said, "Let not the sun go down on your wrath."

God forgives our sins when we ask Him. "My grace is sufficient for you." He will help us have strength of character to forgive others.

We should be somebody in sacrifice! It is not always easy to see someone else get the place you wanted in a church or a club or in your work. Sacrifice for others. God is fair and you will not sacrifice for nothing.

Jesus said, "Whosoever loses his life will save it."

If the young man who took his own life had been busy living for others he would have found life too busy and exciting to think of destroying it.

Be somebody through eternity. That you can do by getting ready along the way.

It is a piteous thing to be
Enlisted in no cause at all,
Unsworn to any heraldry;
To fly no banner from the wall,
Own nothing you would try for,
Or bruise your hands or bleed or die for.

Oh, that were heresy indeed
That all God's pity will not stay for,
And your immortal soul will pay for.

How can you know when you are somebody. When to the very best of your ability, you fill the place in which God has put you. We cannot all be rich nor famous, but we can all know we are here for a cause and to the best of our ability carry out our purpose in life.

9

The Shadow of a Man
(Father's Day)

"He that dwelleth in the secret place of the most High shall abide under the shadow of the Almighty."
— Psalm 91:1

In the last few years we have all become very much aware of the people living in the Eastern part of our world. In the East the shadow of a man has far greater significance than it has in the United States. We pay so little attention to shadows except when we are children.

In India a Brahma will throw his food away if the shadow of an outcast has passed over it. In Acts 5:15 we read: "Insomuch that they brought forth the sick unto the streets, and laid them on beds and couches, that at the least the shadow of Peter passing by might over-shadow some of them."

A man's shadow is the symbol of his influence, in East or West.

Influence is always either good or bad — never neutral. A father should be very careful what kind of shadow he casts on his children, for it either helps or hurts, builds up or tears down, blesses or curses. What a responsibility!

Influence is for the most part irrevocable. After it is past we cannot erase the shadow we have cast on the lives of those about us.

We cannot manipulate influence at will. As children we have often played with our shadows trying to make them tall or fat or to make them go away. We have played games with our hands making shadow animals. Life is not like that. We can't say, "Today I'll be good, tomorrow bad." Influence is like the ray of sunlight; it depends upon the sun. Your influence depends upon your relationship to God.

It is enough to say that it is very serious to cast a bad shadow. Turn to the other side and think of the amazing, far-reaching repercussions of a good life. A good shadow is more important than cleverness, brilliance, or worldly accomplishments.

The shadow of a father and the good or bad it casts upon the lives of those about him depends upon that for which he stands.

Our nation is suffering from the acts of children whose parents did not stand for enough and did not enforce their restrictions.

Fathers have the capacity to stand for something.

I know two little girls who frequently play together. One is the daughter of a teacher and she will not play long without a pencil and a card or paper; she just feels that it is an important part of life even at four years of age.

The other playmate has a mother and two older sisters who do a lot of cooking. While her friend is busy scribbling on her cards the little cook pretends to be making all kinds of pies and cakes. Such is the influence of parents.

When I mention the name, George W. Truett, you think of the builder of a great church.

Mention the name of Jessie James and you think of an outlaw and wild sprees of robbery and other crimes.

When your neighbor, your child, your friend, your boss, looks at you or hears your name called, what do they think? That you live by high standards? That you love others? That you are trustworthy?

The Shadow of a Man (Father's Day)

The father who casts a shadow over a household, over the lives of children, has much to take thought of.

Is the person cursed or blessed on which your shadow falls?

The best way to rebuke evil and exalt righteousness is by your daily example. Your example is worth more than all the money you will make working overtime or at extra jobs.

I like the statement I heard someone say: The hardest job a child faces is learning good manners without seeing any.

BEGIN AT HOME

Do you wish the world were better?
Let me tell you what to do.
Set a watch upon your actions,
Keep them always straight and true.
Rid your mind of selfish motives,
Let your thoughts be clear and high,
You can make a little Eden
Of the sphere you occupy.

— E. W. Wilcox

A CREED

I believe in a fellow that lives
On the square,
That plays the game straight
And tries to be fair,
That keeps himself clean in
Body and mind,
That does a good turn and
Seeks to be kind;
I strive to be like that as
Near as I can,
For Jesus, I think, was that
Kind of a man.

— N. N. Barstow

10

Litter Barrel

"Wherefore seeing we also are compassed about with so great a cloud of witnesses, let us lay aside every weight and the sin which doth so easily beset us, and let us run with patience the race that is set before us."
—Hebrews 12:1

Isn't it fun to take a trip on our modern highways in a good fast car! We ride in ease as we look at new sights and places. But do you know what happens as the day wears on and the trip grows longer. Chewingum wrappers, empty coke bottles, malt glasses—all kinds of waste collects in the car.

Then we see a sign, *Litter Barrel Ahead One Mile.* We begin to think how nice it will be to get all the waste and litter out of the car and make a fresh start. Then we see a sign, *Litter Barrel One-fourth Mile on Right.*

We begin to watch, and soon there it is, all painted and nice, with a little road leading right up to it. We drive up, roll down the window and dispose of all the litter. Now we can drive on for hours feeling clean and refreshed.

Isn't it great to be taking a trip through life! Life, like the car, at times gets all littered up with the wrong things.

We might examine our lives to see if they are filled with the wrong kind of literature, which seems to be available in abundance in almost any direction we look.

Litter Barrel

We may allow our lives to become cluttered with television programs that are not worth the time they consume.

If we are not careful we will spend time attending movies that are not worthy of a Christian's time.

Someone defensively said to me, "The shows, and bad literature also, always let the good guy win in the long run." I once knew a dear old minister who would reply to such a statement by saying, "Do you want to be like a hog and swallow a whole bucket of slop for one small biscuit?"

We need to look for a litter barrel sign and dispose of all the wrong we have gathered about us.

In Ezekiel 33:18, 19 we have the picture of a life before it comes to a litter barrel, and afterward.

"When the righteous turneth from his righteousness, and committeth iniquity, he shall even die thereby.

"But if the wicked turn from his wickedness, and do that which is lawful and right, he shall live thereby."

As a litter barrel sits and waits for you to clean up your car – so a place to dispose of the wrong in your life can be found.

Some people actually turn themselves into litter barrels. They accept all the gossip, the ugly talk, and the filth of life. They sit open mouthed, waiting to begin a grudge against someone who has been their friend. Evil thoughts appeal to them more than the good and kind.

A small boy was riding in the car with his grandmother. When someone they were meeting made a bad error in driving, the little boy uttered a bad curse word.

"Son, where did you learn such an ugly word?"

"From Mr. Brown; he knows lots worse words than that one."

The grandmother tried to make sure her grandson was not a litter barrel for Mr. Brown's filth any longer.

We are never tempted as we drive along the highway to pick up a litter barrel and take it with us. We just want to cast aside our waste and forget where we left it.

Likewise, if we turn ourselves into receptacles for filth and ugliness, people will not care to keep our company.

Hebrews 12:1 reads, "Wherefore seeing we are also compassed about with so great a cloud of witnesses, let us lay aside every weight, and the sin which does so easily beset us, and let us run with patience the race that is set before us."

Jesus offers us forgiveness for our wrong thoughts and attitudes. He will forgive and cleanse our hearts if we will ask Him to. So resolve today to live a cleaner, purer life as you take your trip through life.

Philippians 4:8 is a good motto to accept and follow:

"Finally, brethren, whatsoever things are true, whatsoever things are honest, whatsoever things are pure, whatsoever things are lovely, whatsoever things are of good report; if there be any virtue, and if there be any praise, think on these things."

REAPING THOUGHTS

Every good thought is a flower –
Every bad thought is a thorn –
And we pluck – each fleeting hour –
What we've sown since we were born.

In the garden of our thinking –
Or the thorn field thought has wrought –
From a full life we are reaping,
Or from spent life come to nought.

Ere the babe is thru his nursing,
Ere the boy is made a man,
From within the soul is bursting
With its thought a life to plan.

He who builds with noble thinking
Builds for self a better place,
And his soul from Heaven drinking
Stamps God's image on his face.

– Edward V. Wood

11

Love

"Love never faileth; but whether there be prophecies, they shall fail; whether there be tongues, they shall cease; whether there be knowledge it shall vanish away." – I Corinthians 13:8

Henry Ward Beecher said: "Love is the river of life in this world."

Another wrote:

> "The mind has a thousand eyes,
> And the heart but one;
> Yet the light of a whole life dies
> When love is done."

Love is the power that creates genuine friendships. A wonderful example was that of David and Jonathan. Each loved the other as his own soul.

Fortunate indeed is the person who has a friend like David or Jonathan.

Someone else very aptly said; "We must keep both love and friendship in a state of repair."

Some people only show love and friendship for others when it is convenient; yet a friend loves at all times.

Those who love abundantly and generously live abundantly. They may live in cottages or mansions, but if there is lots of love they are happy.

A newly married couple preparing their first home, be it a one-room efficiency apartment or a fine house, must love abundantly if they would be happy. They must be willing to forget each other's mistakes and think of the good.

One of the most often forgotten things about love is that it is something to give others.

In the days of slavery in America, a wealthy landowner lost his wife. He was left with two small babies. He thought best to send the children to his wife's parents in England. Whom could he send on such a sacred mission? A trusted slave was selected to make the long journey by ship.

The ship ran into trouble and all the passengers were ordered into life boats. The last man left on the ship was the Negro slave. In his arms he held a huge bundle.

"Throw away the bundle and get in quickly. There is room for only you" the sailors called.

The old man pulled back the blanket and revealed the twin babies.

"Take the children and leave me, but tell my master I stayed true to my assignment."

The children were placed in the lifeboat and the slave went down with the ship.

"Love seeketh not its own."

How often, as children, we have quoted the verse, "God is love." This is one of the great truths of the Bible and a glorious fact of the universe.

Love is defined as a state of goodwill, favor, and desire towards a person. God has just such a desire towards His creatures. He wants us to have the best, to succeed and be happy. In order to achieve this we must seek to give love to others, and to tell them of God's love.

The life of every true Christian is a garden where love, joy, peace are grown day by day.

We often judge women by the way they dress, the way they keep house, the friends they have, God looks on the heart of a woman and judges her by what He finds there.

Love

One of our friends adopted a baby. To do so the new mother had to give up her job and remain at home. These new parents had to spend money for things they never thought of before. The little one took constant care; she required food and clothing; costly medical care had to be provided. Yet that home was so much happier after the child came to live there. She brought one gift to give her new parents – love.

Love adds beauty to each life it touches. I have known times when I was in the depths of discouragement, and then a loved one stopped to offer encouragement, giving me strength and courage to go on with my tasks, to succeed.

A soldier lost in Africa during World War II was tempted to give up. The odds seemed so many against finding help and being rescued. Just when it seemed he would die of thirst and hunger, he took from his pocket the picture of his wife and two sons.

"They love me and even now are probably praying for me, I must try again."

So he struggled on and that very evening he saw a fire burning in the distance. When he stumbled into the firelight and fell fainting, kind friends who had been searching for him ministered to his needs. Love won the battle.

Later when revived he said, "Only the look at the picture of my wife and sons gave me courage to keep trying."

Oh, how wonderful the world would be if Christian people would let love rule their lives!

With the world so full of hate and greed, how sweet it is when we meet someone who seems to love others more than self.

Tom came home from school to find the house empty. His mother had gone to the home of a neighbor for a few minutes. He was like all boys after school, hungry! Going to the refrigerator, he started to get some food. A bowl slipped out of his hand and accidently broke into many pieces.

Frightened by the accident, Tom ran to his room and crawled under the bed.

In a few moments the mother came home and saw the broken dish. She began to call "Tom, Tom, where are you?"

The mother cleaned up the mess from the fioor and started to look for Tom.

She looked all over the yard, up and down the street, calling all the time.

Finally in desperation she entered the house and started looking again. Under the bed she saw a little boy who had cried himself to sleep.

"Why didn't you answer, Tom?"

"I didn't think you would love me any more after I had broken the dish," he sobbed.

"Why son, you are worth more to me than all the dishes in the world, I love you."

So we, like little Tom, often run and hide when we have disobeyed God. We stop going to church and Sunday School. We say God does not love us any more. All the time He is calling, calling us to come back to His love and forgiveness.

> When one loves, no service seems too hard,
> For in doing unto others we receive of our reward,
> Love lightens every burden; turns darkness into day;
> Love leads us upward, bids us hope;
> Love guards our lives alway.

12

Thank God for Life
(Thanksgiving)

"Oh, that men would praise the Lord for his goodness, and for his wonderful works to the children of men."
– Psalm 107:8

There's something in the atmosphere
Around this magic time of year,
That thrills the hearts of men,
And sort of sets the blood astir,
And makes the pulses fairly purr,
From which no doubt you will infer –
Thanksgiving's here again.

– J. E. Hungersford

How we Americans do love Thanksgiving time! It is a time of remembrance in our personal lives. We recall the blessings of the year just past; we feel new gratitude for the mercies of the present.

As a nation we remember the Pilgrims and the motives which impelled them to come to America.

Every person should be thankful for his life.

James 4:14 reads: "What is your life?"

Have you ever taken time to thank God that you were allowed to be born, to come into this world a living, vital person? We should be thankful for just the fact of life.

We should be thankful for life because it means self. Life is something wonderful, unfathomable, and mysterious.

God did not give us just the fact of our life but He gave us our five senses: seeing, hearing, feeling, tasting, smelling.

Have you met a blind man lately? Did you not in your heart say, "Thank you God for letting me see."

Sitting sometimes today, in your car, your home, or office, did you hear sweet music and stop to thank God for the gift of hearing?

Then besides the senses we should thank God for other things. What about the ability to work, to hold a job and draw a pay check? Work seems to be unpopular among some elements of our society, but we as Christians should thank our Heavenly Father for the ability and privilege of work.

Life is so wonderful and so mysterious, yet at times we need to talk it over with a higher power. Thank God for prayer. Prayer releases us from our burden of sin, helps us find comfort in trouble, and gives us renewed strength for each day.

When night comes and we close our eyes in restful sleep we should thank God for the ability to sleep.

> I thank thee, heavenly Father, for the simple gift of birth,
> The sheer delight of drawing breath in this good world of Thine.
> Each year has brought a deeper sense of all that life is worth,
> And even pain and weakness cannot mar Thy wise design.

What is your life?

Will you make it a life for which to be thankful?

Someone has written, "Life is a soul's career in a body."

We have no way to control the number of years allotted to us for living on this earth, but we can control how we fill those years with good or bad.

What is your life? Life is a pursuit. We are always reaching out for something. Women reach out for pretty clothes, better furniture, better homes, comforts for their families.

Men reach out for money and the good they can accomplish with it. They pursue better education for their families, better homes, larger bank accounts.

How thankful we should be for life, not only for the fact of life itself, but for the wonderful lives we are permitted to live! We have seen the world come alive in so many scientific ways. We have enjoyed ease and comforts beyond the wildest imaginings of our Pilgrim fathers. We are people, alive and able to use power and influence. Our lives are not the lives of animals. We are given that breath of God, a spark never to be quenched. We are immortal and we should forever give thanks to God for providing a way for us to spend eternity in Heaven.

We should be thankful for life at this particular time. A small boy watched as his older sister and brother prepared for school. The long hours at home alone seemed unfair to him. He ran to his mother and asked, "Mommie, why didn't you borned me sooner so I could go to school?"

We face a glorious future. We should look up and be grateful for the gift of life. Almost anyone can get an education today. Even adults can attend night classes. The darkness of ignorance need never envelop us as long as we are free to read and listen.

What is your life? It is a gift from God. So you should be thankful and strive to fill your life with quality living.

> Lord, I am glad for the great gift of living —
> Glad for Thy days of sun and rain;
> Grateful for joy, with an endless thanksgiving,
> Grateful for laughter — and grateful for pain.
>
> Sun, bloom and blossom, O Lord, I remember,
> The dream of the spring and its joys I recall;
> But now in the silence and pain of November,
> Lord, I give thanks to Thee, giver of all.
>
> — Charles Hanson Towne

Some people fail in life because they never come face to

face with the realization that their life is something precious and important, something for which to be thankful.

Because God has given us life we should determine to spend the period of time allotted us on earth in the most useful way possible. Daily we should seek to help others, to improve our own station in life, and by example to point others to the Giver of all good gifts.

When you are aware someone has done you a favor, you think, What can I do for him in return?

Two boys in a small village determined to go to a city to find work and, as they pictured it, success.

They found jobs and were soon caught up in the whirl of making a living in a large city. One of the boys found a church and attended every Sunday. He met people just like the ones he had known at home and his life did become a success. The other boy thought his friend foolish to go to church. He spent his Sundays prowling about over the city and became friends with some boys who led him deeper and deeper into sin. His life became a failure and a waste.

What is your life? You can make it a success by being thankful to God and to your parents for the gift of life. A person who is truly thankful seeks to be a person who renders service.

The Psalmist cried out: "What shall I render unto the Lord, for all his benefits toward me?"

13

The Grace of Having Enough

"And Esau said, I have enough, my brother; keep that thou hast unto thyself." – Genesis 33:9

"Take, I pray thee, my blessing that is brought to thee; because God hath dealt graciously with me, and because I have enough." – Genesis 33:11

In the verses above we find two brothers who have not met for many years. One wishes to give a very generous gift to the other. We find each declaring, "I have enough."

How strange those words sound in this world today. It seems we seldom meet a person who is satisfied with what God has given him. Everyone wants more.

Someone has said the modern Christian will be surprised when he gets to heaven and finds the angels are not trying to get more than their fellow angels.

It would seem that there is very little of the grace of having enough in our world today.

How we do enjoy being with a person who is content and happy with his lot in life. A person who is truly content and grateful for what he has, is really the possessor of great spiritual riches.

For many years I attended a church where an evening meal for the workers and their children was served on Wednesday.

A junior boy I remember so well, Dave, always rushed to get far ahead of his mother in the line. Then he filled his plate to overflowing. I have often seen him eat four hot rolls. To those of us sitting near him would come the question, "Does he ever get enough?"

At times we would offer Dave things from our plates, and he always accepted and devoured what was offered. I never heard him say, "I have enough."

In youth we see people who just can't seem to get enough of living. They rush madly from one activity to another.

We have all known girls who reached an age when they just could not get enough clothes to satisfy them, or boys who felt they just had to play one more ball game before they could quit for the night.

It seems to be human nature to want more of whatever we happen to be interested in at the moment.

Business men want more business; women want more furniture and knickknacks for their houses; we all want more than we have.

To develop the grace of having enough we must first examine ourselves and see what we really want from life.

Those of us who have passed the bloom of youth should have a better sense of values than we had twenty years ago.

We know we are going to have enough to eat and enough to wear, but why are we then so often discontented. Why can't we say, "I have enough"?

The first step in realizing the grace of having enough is to know and believe the Scripture verse which says: "Every good gift and every perfect gift is from above, and cometh down from the Father of lights" (James 1:17).

If we are truly God's children we will rest in the faith that He gives us that which we need when we need it.

Do you remember the widow in the Bible who shared her meager supply of meal with the Prophet of God? Each day there was meal enough for her needs.

If she had been a modern-day woman she would have complained and said: "My neighbor has more than I; why can't I have some fresh vegetables and maybe a nice roast of lamb?"

The widow was content with what God supplied.

Some things of which we should want more are God's power and grace bestowed upon us. May we never say we have enough. He has an overabundant supply, we have but to ask for it.

Christ's love and forgiveness is something else we can be assured of in an overabundant supply.

I want to tell you the story of a lady who decided that for a whole week she would complain of nothing, no one, and just be content. She laughingly told her family they were going to have C-week (Contentment-Week).

The teen-aged children were so used to hearing their mother complain that they went into gales of laughter at her announcement.

The very first morning of C-Week the washing machine refused to work properly. Quick words of complaint rushed to the mother's lips but she stifled them and went to call a repair man.

As she and the daughter wrung out the clothes and emptied the machine so the man could repair it, she told stories of her girlhood when they had a hand-operated washing machine. The water to fill it had to be carried from a well, and washing was a long day's chore. The daughter saw her mother in a new light and each loved and respected the other more by the time the washing was finished.

When it was time for the evening meal the mother realized she had forgotten to buy bread.

The son started to complain, but then remembered it was C-Week. He jumped up and told his mother, "I'll ride my bike to the store and be back by the time you are ready and seated."

When all were at last at the table the father was told of

some of the day's adventures. All were laughing and eating happily.

Three years later the son was called into military service. Often the family prayed for his safety.

One day he wrote in a letter: "I could not stand the terror of war if you had not taught me long ago during our C-Week that God gives us enough strength for each day as it comes."

That night the mother and father prayed together for the loved one far away. "Father, we have enough of all life's comforts; please take care of our loved one so far away."

How much better we would all feel if we developed the grace of having enough. We must share God's message if we would truly have enough love in our hearts.

> Life is a gift to be used every day
> Not to be smothered and hidden away;
> It isn't a joy to be sipped now and then
> And promptly put back in a dark place again.
> Life is a gift that the humblest may boast of
> And one that the humblest may well make the most of.
> Get out and live it each hour of the day,
> Wear it and use it as much as you may;
> Don't keep it in niches and corners and grooves,
> You'll find that in service its beauty improves.

14

Cheer Up!

"Why art thou cast down, O my soul? and why art thou disquieted within me? Hope thou in God; for I shall yet praise him, who is the health of my countenance, and my God." – Psalm 42:11

While sitting in front of a mirror in the beauty shop, waiting for my operator to start working on my hair, I was startled by a girl who stopped by my side.

"Cheer up," she said, "It can't be that bad."

I had not realized until then that my face was all gloomy as I had been observing many new grey hairs, and just about as many new lines of old age.

Why was I despondent? Was it because I didn't look the way I had twenty years ago? After her startling statement I began to ask myself questions.

Do I want to stop living just because I am growing older? My friends are also growing older. Do I want them to go about complaining about their age? No!

We should all be so glad God has given us all the years we have had to enjoy, to make mistakes and make new starts.

Every person in the world, regardless of his age, is growing older. As I took another look in the mirror I gave a silent prayer of thanks that God had allowed me to live this long.

When my beauty operator started shampooing my hair

she asked me why I was smiling. My outlook had changed quickly when I counted a few blessings.

Some people suffer from spiritual despondency. They look at the wickedness running rampant in the world and feel all is lost.

Some suffer from spiritual despondency because they have suffered earthly misfortunes or bereavements.

Others suffer from spiritual despondency because they have allowed sin to fill their lives. The burden of their sins makes them sad.

Cheer up, whatever the cause of your despondency. As our Scripture verse suggests, "Hope thou in God." A firm trust in God will lighten any load and give us grace to bear our burdens.

We should trust God because He is so good to us. Stop and look at all His goodness. Are you well? Are you close to those you love? Are you able to worship when and as you please? What does the future hold?

All these questions can be answered with joy and thanksgiving if we are truly God's children.

Psalm 90:12 reads, "So teach us to number our days that we may apply our hearts unto wisdom."

I read the story of a blind man in Florida. Not only was he blind but his body was twisted and suffering with the dread disease arthritis.

This man does not let all his troubles keep him from having friends. He makes calls for his church and invites people to attend services.

Many people make calls, even people who are handicapped; but this great Christian always says: "Hello there! It's a wonderful day."

How our outlook would change if we would greet each friend with the statement, "It's a wonderful day!"

How can we cheer up? We can keep learning. Learning

keeps the mind fresh and alert. A man past seventy-five was asked how he kept so young and lively in spirit.

He pointed to a tree growing near his doorway.

"You see that tree grows a little new wood each year; that is the secret of its life. I plan to learn something new each day of my life."

How can we cheer up? By making new friends. The friends we have are fine and good, but we need to meet people with fresh ideas. We must be open to friendship if we would be cheerful. Loneliness leads to a grumpy disposition. Replenish your friendship list with a child. Children bring cheer and goodwill wherever they go.

I had a friend in her late thirties. She was a widow with one child. Each time she was asked to serve the church in some way she made excuses. She was too tired after working in an office all day. Her little girl needed her.

Then the pastor touched her heart with a message and she offered to work for the Extension Department of the church. Soon she had a wonderful department organized and a number of people working under her supervision. She grew to love the people who worked with her. Through one of the workers she met a bachelor and was married.

She was often heard to say that God brought her happiness when she started thinking about others in place of herself.

There is something useful for every person to do if he keeps in close touch with Christ.

IT'S YOU

You say the world looks gloomy,
  The skies are grim and gray
The night has lost its quiet,
  You fear the coming day.

The world is what you make it;
  The sky is gray or blue
Just as your soul may paint it;
  It isn't the world – it's you.

Clear up the clouded vision,
  Clean out the foggy mind;
The clouds are always passing
  And each is silver lined.

The world is what you make it –
  Then make it bright and true;
And when you say it's gloomy
  It isn't the world – it's you.

15

True Riches

"There is that maketh himself rich, yet hath nothing: there is that maketh himself poor, yet hath great riches."
—Proverbs 13:7

Sometimes we miss counting our best riches because we are looking for some great, outstanding gift. Yet it is often the small everyday blessings that make up the true riches of life.

Sometimes a friend or loved one goes an extra mile for us and we fail to realize what a blessing it is.

On Sunday night after church a teen-age girl came to my husband and asked him to take his keys and go with her to the Activities Building across the street so she could look for her coat.

The girl, her mother, my husband and myself all went to the building, all the way to the basement, looking for the coat. No coat could we find.

The mother and her daughter left and went home. My husband was very tired but he knew she needed her coat for school that week. He went back to the main church building and searched until he finally found the coat high up on a shelf in the choir room. Some mischevious child had put it there.

I call a friend who will spend strength and time like that a blessing of true riches.

For youth, a true kind of riches is a noble purpose for living and getting ready for the future. For small children, true riches is having the love and attention of good parents. For adults, true riches is being able to live in peace and joy, serving those we love. To live a truly abundant life one must have someone to love.

There is a song that goes; "It's love, it's love, it's love that makes the world go around."

Well, it is love that fills the heart of man with true riches. We were made to love and are not complete until we have set our affections on someone.

It is sad to see a person who is hungry for food, but food can be bought or begged. A person starved for love has a greater problem.

I once knew a beautiful woman who neglected her husband. She was not untrue to him. She saw that the home was kept perfectly and even kept his books at the place of business. She just never took time to talk to him or listen to his problems. She would always put him off if he started to tell her something.

For two weeks he tried to tell her that he wanted to go to a doctor for a checkup.

"You can wait until after inventory," she kept saying.

She never bothered to ask where he hurt or why he felt he should see a doctor.

One morning he failed to get up. Going to his room she found him cold in death.

For days all she could say over and over was, "Death is so final! I never took time to tell him I loved him."

Close friends felt the man had literally died from lack of love and attention.

Rich indeed is the child who is often found cuddled on a parent's lap. The place where he lives may be small, but there is no riches to be compared to the love of a parent with time for a caress and a game.

Money will buy many things – comforts, travel, large homes, but money will not buy true love. Only the person who has someone who truly loves him is rich.

An important lawyer in the early days of Dallas, Texas, found himself accused in a lawsuit. He was innocent but he had to prove his innocence. Many of the people who had clustered around him before now stayed away. One man from far out in the country could not get to the trial but he daily sent a letter of encouragement and love to the lawyer.

Later when the lawyer's name was cleared he made a trip to the country to visit his friend.

"Each day when things seemed to look the blackest your letter would arrive," the lawyer told him. "Then I would know I had one real friend, and fight on."

In the month of February we think a lot about love and those who love us. We plan little surprises for the children and grandchildren so they will know we love them in a special way.

I Corinthians 13:13 reads in one of the popular new versions: "In a word, there are three things that last forever: faith, hope, and love, but the greatest of them all is love."

If you want to be loved you must be lovable! Do we want true riches enough to work at loving others? Too often we take love for granted until it is too late, then we too cry in anguish: "Death is so final."

MY HUSBAND

He never says, "I love you so,"
As I somehow thought he would,
But if I ask, he says, "You know I do,
That's understood."

He never says he likes my dress
Or likes the tune I'm playing,
But if I ask, he answers, "Yes,
That goes without my saying."

I ask him, "Will your love for me
Be always true and steady?"
He sighs and says, so wearily,
"I've told you that already."

"For better or for worse," and more
The kind old parson chanted,
I don't know which I took John for,
But he took me for granted.

—John's wife (Unknown)

TRUE HAPPINESS

True happiness grows at your own fireside,
And abundantly blossoms there.
When those of the home in contentment abide,
And are grateful for God's love and care.

Now you cannot pluck from your neighbor's yard
The sweet joy you feel you need,
For it has to grow, though you may think it hard,
Deep within as your own thought and deed.

— J. T. Bolding

16

Why Blame Others?

"According as he hath chosen us in him before the foundation of the world, that we should be holy and without blame before him in love." – Ephesians 1:4

When something goes amiss and there is trouble and unnecessary expense, we are prone to blame someone or something for the mistake.

The *Houston Chronicle,* during the early days of the space rockets, told a strange story of a rocket that was launched and destroyed. To destroy the rocket meant a loss of $18,000,000. Someone or something had to take the blame for such a great loss. The trouble was attributed to failure of a computer.

The rocket veered off course slightly, but a "bar," or hyphen, was supposed to tell the computer that all was yet well. However, for some reason, the hyphen was omitted so the computer started sending corrections. The rocket became "confused" and headed off in wrong directions and had to be destroyed. All because something this - long was left out.

We often talk about the terrible condition our world is in. We blame the politicians, the educators and the foreigners.

Do you ever stop to think you might be able to help make the world a better place! You might be just the "hyphen" that would direct some young person to a better course. Why blame others until we have given our best in love and work to make the world better?

Remember the story of Jonah? Christians often hear the call, "Go for me to Nineveh today."

When we come to the fork in the road, like Jonah we turn aside and say, "Wait until tomorrow; I want to go this way today."

Oh, the joy and blessings experienced by Christians who do not wait to blame someone for their shortcomings but follow willingly where God leads.

God often leads us to do hard things or go to strange places to win the lost but He will take care of us as we go.

We often find ourselves blaming others for the troubles about us instead of asking God what we can do to make things better.

I read a story in the paper of a woman who had a heart attack while driving her car. As she slumped over the wheel her car ran into the car ahead. When the man in the front car saw her condition he immediately administered first aid. The damage to his car was quickly forgotten when he saw the opportunity to save a life.

Are you blaming others because your home life is not as happy as it should be? Have you tried your best in love to make it better?

Why blame others anyway, even if we know them to be at fault? Why not just do our bit to make the world a better place?

Is there some person living near you needing direction and encouragement? Don't turn aside as Jonah did; try to help them.

My class sent a substantial offering to a mission church in the North. We received only one brief letter of thanks. Vainly we waited for another letter telling of all the wonderful good our money had accomplished. When no further word arrived, I said to myself, "Hereafter we will send our money to someone who appreciates us."

Six months later a letter arrived. The mission pastor had been working day and night, teaching school in order to live and caring for a church full-time. I felt so ashamed as I read of his struggles. Who was I to have blamed him for not writing sooner?

What should I have done in place of finding fault? I should have prayed for the man and his work. Prayer availeth much. We can all pray!

When tempted to blame someone for some shortcoming this week, just ask yourself if you can do something to make things better. Why blame others? Be your best for God and you will not see others faults so clearly.

THE SERMON THAT IS YOU

Who can tell what good may come
From little things you do? –
Who can tell who's listening now
To the sermon that is you? –

Trusting friends see where you go
For pleasure and for play –
They watch you live throughout the week,
And hear the things you say –

And knowing you are good and strong,
Their faith in you still stands –
They'd sooner take advice from you
Than any other man. –

The little children watch you pass,
And oft they're heard to say: –
"I want to be just like that man
When I grow up some day." –

So don't you think it worth the while
To choose your words with care,
Since little folks around you
Are watching everywhere?

Don't you think it is much wiser
To watch the way you walk,—
Lest tender souls may injured be
By careless tread and talk?—

Who can tell what good may come
From little things you do?—
Who can tell who's listening now
To the sermon that is you?—

—Edward V. Wood

17

The Garden of Our Lives

"For lo, the winter is past, the rain is over and gone; The flowers appear on the earth; the time of the singing of birds is come, and the voice of the turtle is heard in our land" — Song of Solomon 2:11, 12

Each person is given a garden to tend,
  Whether for one year or three-score and ten.
Have you planted flowers rare
  Or are you growing thistles there?

Every day of life is a day for planting in the garden of our lives. The question we face is, What are we planting there?

In the school I attended was a tall and graceful girl. She excelled in almost everything she chose to do. After graduation she went to Africa as a missionary.

When she returned home on furlough after five years, I eagerly went to hear her speak.

She was not so beautiful as when she had left school. Her hair was turning prematurely grey. Her face was brown from the African sun. Her hands were rough from much hard work.

As she talked we were transported to her field of labor. We saw the people in need; we rejoiced when she told of winning some for Christ. She seemed to be plucking flowers from the garden of her life and holding them out for us to enjoy also.

As we look at our own lives let us think about the kind of flowers we are growing. Are they flowers rare of blessings for others, or are we merely growing thistles?

The first and most beautiful flower in every life should be a firm belief in Jesus Christ. With that for a background, almost any garden of life will be successful.

The second flower to make our garden beautiful should be the flower of service. All people are happier when they serve others. A person may not be physically beautiful, but the person who serves lives a beautiful life.

When sunset falls upon your day
And fades from out the West.
When business cares are put away
And you lie down to rest.
The measure of the day's success,
Or failure, may be told
In terms of human happiness
And not in terms of gold.

Is there beside some hearth tonight
More joy because you wrought?
Does someone face the bitter fight
With courage you have taught?
Is something added to the store
Of human happiness?
If so the day that now is o'er
Has been a real success.

The garden of our lives grows slowly day by day, through the years. Every kind deed we do, every lesson we learn helps our garden grow.

Each touch of another life on ours, each book we read, each influence that impresses us adds something to our garden of life.

The third flower in our garden should be a flower of praise, praise for others. If we develop the habit of praising others we will make our own life more beautiful.

If you were busy being kind,
Before you knew it, you would find

You'd soon forget to think 'twas true
That someone was unkind to you.

If you were busy being glad,
And cheering people who are sad,
Although your heart might ache a bit,
You'd soon forget to notice it.

If you were busy being good,
And doing just the best you could,
You'd not have time to blame some man,
Who's doing just the best he can.

If you were busy being right,
You'd find yourself too busy quite
To criticize some neighbor long
Because he's busy being wrong.

Another tall, beautiful flower in our garden of life is the flower of purity. And life looks marred and ugly without the glow of purity.

One day I asked a little boy what he wanted to be when he grew up. You would never guess his answer!

"I want to be alive!" he told me.

Don't we all want to be alive? But is that enough?

No, we want to be doing something, planting beautiful flowers in our garden of life.

Have you ever noticed how a true gardner likes to share plants with others?

Think of a whole cluster of good cheer flowers we can pluck from our garden and share. Flowers of smiles, happy greetings, optimistic viewpoint, kind words, encouragement.

Back of our good cheer flowers stands a border of the flower called compassion. We must have compassion for others if we would share the flowers growing in our own garden of life.

One lovely thing about a garden is that we are always dreaming how beautiful it will be when the plants have grown larger or are in bloom. So life must have flowers of ambition and dreams for the future.

Over fifty years ago a little poem appeared in many first grade readers;

> Bite off more than you can chew;
>   Then chew it.
> Plan more work than you can do;
>   Then do it.
> Hitch your wagon to a star,
>   Keep your seat
> And there you are:
>   Go to it.

We have to constantly tend our garden of life if we would keep it growing and flowering with the flowers we have mentioned. All along the way we will find new plants to add to our garden.

> God loaned me life and I must pay
> Him back a portion of each day
> In loving service; I must give
> A part of every hour I live
> In thoughtful, kindly deeds to others
> Who are my sisters and my brothers.
>
> God loaned me coins I may not spend
> For any wasteful, selfish end.
> They are a trust that I must hold
> As sacred. All the world's bright gold
> Belongs to Him, and in my spending
> I must repay His gracious lending.
>
> God put His love within my heart,
> A love I ever must impart
> To a world in desperate need of care.
> All things God gave me I must share.
> This is the stewardship of living;
> A spontaneous and joyous giving.

What makes a person great? Not what is under his hat, but what is growing in his heart. Do something about the garden of your life!

A traveler once stopped at a country store near Hannibal,

Missouri, where the great humorist and writer Mark Twain spent the formative years of his life.

The visitor asked the proprietor of the store if he knew Mark Twain.

"Sure I knew him," came the prompt reply. "And I know just as many stories as he did, too, only difference is, he writ 'em down."

Don't stand and be jealous of the person who "writ 'em down." Go out and plant beautiful flowers in your own life.

18

The Business of Life

"For whosoever will save his life shall lose it; but whosoever shall lose his life for my sake and the gospel's, the same shall save it." – Mark 8:35

"For what shall it profit a man, if he shall gain the whole world, and lose his own soul?" – Mark 8:36

In the world of business a man may sometimes make a big profit or he may operate for a time at a loss. Some smart businessmen will take a small loss today to make a greater profit in the future.

In the business of men's spiritual lives we see people who refuse to take the loss of a few earthly pleasures today in order to have the great blessing of eternal life tomorrow.

A popular teacher in our town made the statement that life consisted of five things: time, energy, thought, ability, and money.

The fact is, we may have all five of the elements she mentioned and still fail if we do not commit our spiritual welfare to God through faith in Jesus Christ.

The business of life is the biggest business in which anyone will ever be involved.

One day the janitor of a large church was asked how he could tolerate being ordered about by so many demanding people.

"Well, you see it is this way," he replied, "I just throws it in neutral and lets them push me around."

We cannot make a success of the business of our life if we, "just throw it in neutral and let them push us around." We must have definite goals to reach. We must have plans and ambitions for reaching those goals. A good businessman is not satisfied to make just as much this year as he made last. He wants to improve, to go forward.

Big businessmen spend money finding out the trends of the times. They sometimes pay analysts to study their business and make suggestions.

People who take the business of life seriously will go to the greatest analyst of all. His advice can be found on the pages of the Bible. To read and follow that device means assured success in the business of life.

We are living in an age when even the poorest people can buy stock in the stock market. Upon payment of an initial amount, they may join an investment group and make monthly purchases. The more they start with and the more they can pay each month the more stock they own.

In the business of life we must also make an initial investment; then each day of our lives add to our investment.

If we give Christ all of our heart it will not be hard to live for Him each day.

"For what will it profit a man, if he shall gain the whole world, and lose his own soul?"

In one of our local high schools there was a boy, who was a model pupil. His grades were above average and he was always cooperative with the pupils and teachers.

Suddenly one morning his character completely changed. When the teacher asked him to put a problem on the black board he replied, "I will not!"

The teacher was astonished, "Did I misunderstand you?"

"No, I will not go to the board," he replied.

She asked him to step out into the hall so she could talk to him in private.

"You are one of my best pupils," she pleaded, "why are you acting like this?"

"I just am."

"I will have to take you to the principal's office."

So the two went to the principal's office and the boy, when questioned by a higher authority, still replied, "I will not."

"I will have to call your father," the principal said in sorrow.

"Good!" He brightened up. "He hasn't had time to talk to me in two years. Maybe if I am a bad boy he will."

The father was called and counseled to see that his son received the love and companionship he needed.

Look for a moment at your life. How you invest your life is the most important question you face on earth. You may make financial investments and lose money but if you are industrious you can earn more money. But you have only one life to invest and if you waste it you can never get it back. It is gone to a point of no return.

Face the facts – and the future. Are you choosing the right authority for the investing of your life? Are you spending time in service for the Master or are you expecting the first investment you made when you accepted Christ as your Saviour to be enough?

Sometimes there will pass through a town some person with counterfeit stocks and bonds to sell. He will be so clever with his sales talk that many good people will be duped into investing with him. After collecting his profits he disappears and people find they have lost all they invested.

Examine your life; are you a counterfeit Christian? If Christ could die on the cross for lost people, can't we carry the cross He assigns to us? Do we owe Him any less?

TRY IT! WILL YA?

If you're feeling kinda poorly,
I'll tell you what you do:

If you will you can
Find some troubled man
Who's a lot worse off than you.

Give him a lift – a helping hand;
Cheer him along his way.
Thus meet his need;
Bid him God's speed;
You'll have a better day.

Seek out a friend who's kinda low;
Lift him with a kindly word;
Your spirit will soar
On high once more,
Like a care-free, singing bird.

When you pass the blind and the crippled,
Loosen the old purse string;
Toss in a buck;
Thus change your luck;
See what giving will bring.

Look about for someone who needs you;
Take time – meet someone's need;
You'll feel mighty good,
Like you really should,
When you do a good deed.

So when in the dumps you are feeling,
I'll tell you what you do:
If you will you can
Find some troubled man
Who's a lot worse off than you.

– Edward V. Wood

19

House-cleaning Time

"And they that be wise shall shine as the brightness of the firmament; and they that turn many to righteousness as the stars for ever and ever" – Daniel 12:3

In our sandy West Texas it is a custom to clean house in the spring after we think all the sand storms are past. Often we will have a few days of very nice weather and all the women will wash windows and clean rugs and floors. The men will work just as diligently on the flower beds and cutting away of the dead grass. All this activity is lots of hard work and yet we enjoy it.

All too often we have been fooled by a nice day and the sand comes blowing back so thick we can't see past our own fences. All the work will have to be repeated.

Picture windows have been very popular the last twenty years and everyone felt he just had to have a picture window. What a task to clean these windows and keep them clear and sparkling!

Like our houses, our lives often get all filled up with the sands of sin and selfishness and we need a time of spiritual housecleaning.

When we start to clean our windows it is so much easier if one stays outside the house and polishes while one remains inside. When each can see the other without any smudges or streaks between, we say that window is finished.

Think about the picture windows of your life. Is God on the outside trying to see your heart through a lot of smudges of sin?

Not long ago I made a visit in a home where there is a lingering case of terminal illness. My impression was that I had never been in a house so clean before. I have visited in many larger houses with finer furniture but that house just seemed so perfectly clean and polished.

As soon as my visit was finished I hurried home and, changing into other clothes, started cleaning my house.

When someone looks at your daily life is he inspired by the purity and beauty of cleanliness he sees there? Does he in turn want to live better because of your example?

A good housewife hates dirt and wants to get rid of it. Our Heavenly Father hates sin. He hates it so much He sent Christ, His only Son, to make a way for us to escape from sin.

Look at your window, do you see it all clouded over with selfishness? Just as an earthly parent hates to see selfishness in his children, so God hates to see His children selfish and greedy.

In West Texas we cannot help getting sand on our windows and in our houses. So Christians cannot help getting some sin in their lives because they live in a sinful world.

Does living in a sinful world excuse us from cleaning up our lives? No. At all times we should be trying to keep the glass in the window of our hearts so clean we can see God.

The first way to begin is to confess our sins and ask forgiveness for them.

"If we confess our sins, he is faithful and just to forgive us our sins, and to cleanse us from all unrighteousness" (I John 1:9).

After we have cleared away the sins in our life we must work to challenge other people to follow our example. We cannot do this if we merely *look* pure and clean, we must *be* clean. Each little corner of our hearts must be polished and shined in the love of God.

I used to visit a lady who had a saying: "Sweep it under the rug and come on."

Often I wanted to peep under her rug and see if she really did sweep her dirt under the rug. People can tell in our lives if we just sweep our sins and shortcomings out of sight. We must get rid of them completely. Of course, like the sandstorms, they will come back and our hearts will have to be cleaned again because we are not perfect.

To keep a clean house we need brooms and mops and dust cloths.

To keep a clean Christian life we also need some equipment. One of the most necessary items is a prayer time. We must talk to God if we are to keep His light shining in our lives. We should not pray only for our own lives but for those to whom we witness.

Then there is the Bible! The Bible should be a daily companion. Even if you have time to read just a few pages or verses it will help you keep the right outlook on life.

Another great instrument in keeping our spiritual house clean is the assembling of ourselves together in the Lord's house.

Then there is the giving of our means and time to bring in the Kingdom. We give to those we love, so our love for God can be measured by our gifts.

How is your spiritual house this morning?

Whenever things go wrong for me,
  I feel so all alone,
And in my heart I tell myself
  The fault is all my own.

I wonder what there is in me
  That draws the luck I get,
And why I do so many things
  I surely must regret.

House-cleaning Time

I try to change my way of life;
  I start anew, and then,
Before the sun goes down, I make
  The same mistakes again.

There must be some solution to
  This puzzle of my life
And some successful remedy
  For my eternal strife.

I bow my head and ask the Lord
  To tell me what to do,
To fill my life with great success
  And make me happy, too.

Then in my heart I hear Him speak
  Of Jesus' love for me,
Of peace that comes by trusting Him,
  Of how He set me free.

Forgive me, Lord, for seeking praise
  From men who cannot see,
And through Thy Spirit teach me how
  To live my life for Thee.

– James Bolding, Jr.

20

Trees
(Spring or Fall)

"And he looked up, and said, I see men as trees, walking." – Mark 8:24

Can there be anyone who doesn't enjoy and like a beautiful tree? Not long ago I read an article in which the writer advised people buying or building new houses to save enough capital for the planting of trees around the new place.

A friend, who had just moved into a new place proudly showed us his trees. They were fifteen feet high and had cost him a large amount of money.

"I am too old to wait for trees to grow," he explained "so I bought some already large enough to be beautiful."

Most of us prefer to plant small trees and watch them mature through the years.

In a number of places in the Bible man is compared to a tree.

"And he shall be like a tree planted by the rivers of water, that bringeth forth his fruit in his season" (Ps. 1:3).

Tree-worship has been common all over the world. Adherents of religions believed trees to have spirits. Sacred groves were found in ancient Canaan. Jupiter was a deity especially connected with the oak tree.

When Christ came His followers learned the way of salvation in Christ and ceased worshiping natural objects.

Trees (Spring or Fall)

"Who his own self bare our sins in his own body on the tree, that we, being dead to sins, should live unto righteousness: by whose stripes ye were healed" (I Peter 2:24).

Jesus had been asked by the friends of a blind man to restore his sight. After Jesus had touched his eyes He asked the man if he could see. The man replied that he could see men as trees walking.

Jesus healed many people by just a word, but this man seemed to need help in believing. Jesus could see his heart and knew what was best for him.

Things were not clear for him at first; his vision was blurred. Are we not often the same way? We want to believe Christ can answer our prayers, fill our needs, but we see things only as trees walking.

The man could tell they were moving; but he knew trees did not walk about. He could see they were erect so he said he saw men as trees walking.

Christ does not do things by halves. He put His hands on the man's eyes again and he could see clearly.

Perhaps sometimes our lives seem unsettled and we see God's will as a blur because we need another contact with Christ. We need His hands upon our lives.

How can we get Christ to touch our hearts again and make them clear and plain?

First we must come into His presence in prayer and ask for help. Then, when we see clearly His will for us, we must go forth to carry out His purpose in our lives.

In Matthew 12:33 we find man compared to a tree: "Either make the tree good and his fruit good; or else make the tree corrupt, and his fruit corrupt, for a tree is known by his fruit."

It is Christ's will for us to see clearly and to serve completely as He directs us.

Christianity is not new, we need to see it with new faith. Christ will reward our faith by giving us better sight and understanding.

A boys father, explaining the eclipse of the moon said, "The sun is still shining just as always; the moon is also there, but the earth gets between them."

The love of our Heavenly Father is always shining. We are here to receive it but at times we let the earth come between us and we cannot see clearly. We must ask Christ to touch our lives again.

TREES

From you were built the slender masted ships
Which sailed across the deep, blue sea,
To bring explorers on discovery trips
And settle our forebears so free.

Your lumber housed against the stormy blast;
Your wood-fed fires drove out the cold,
And warmed the young until grown up at last,
Then comforted the very old.

Your shade protects from summer's burning sun;
Your fruit the hungry oft has fed;
Upon your branches clamber boys in fun;
Beneath, tired campers make a bed.

With hillsides decked in rich and restful greens,
You often bless man's weary eyes,
And edge his path with many lovely scenes
From birth until at last he dies.

—J. T. Bolding

21

The Law of Prayer

"Ask and it shall be given you." – Luke 11:9
"Ye have not because ye ask not." – James 4:2

The first Scripture verse given above is one of the most precious promises in the Bible. It is the condition for our receiving any good gift from God. God has a treasure-house full of wonderful blessings. Picture the doors of that treasure house as locked. We can knock and they will be opened when we pray. Many times we see others receiving blessings and we wonder why they did not come to us.

James wrote, "Ye have not because ye ask not." The law of prayer is simple. Ask and receive!

If God loves us and wants us to have blessings, why do we need to pray at all?

There is a great mystery about prayer. Those who have the greatest need so often do not ask. Wicked people, indifferent people, unbelieving people, need so much, yet they fail to ask for help.

When God made man He gave him freedom of his human will. So we must submit that will to God and ask for help.

When we pray to God we can be sure He will listen. He wants to hear our requests.

There is something about the very act of asking a favor of God that relaxes and encourages us. Yes, prayer is a mystery!

Yet every prayer is a knock on the door of heaven and each knock brings a blessing.

"Ask and it shall be given you; seek, and ye shall find; knock, and it shall be opened unto you" (Matt. 7:7).

How can we expect to have our lives filled with the Holy Spirit unless we spend some time in prayer each day?

THE POWER OF PRAYER

If we pray not, how aimlessly we sail
  The seas of life. No compass points us on.
We trust false gleams that shine awhile, to fail;
  But shadows gloom ahead, no rising dawn.

His soul is given wings who learns to pray;
  Swiftly and surely he can Godward fly;
Courageously can meet each dangerous day
  And foes without, within, he can defy.

We pray in darkness and a light appears;
  We pray when lost, to find our Father's hand,
True to His promise, wipes away our tears,
  Even while dwelling in this pilgrim land.

While we are crying "Help my unbelief!"
  The soul feels life beyond this life so brief.

In March of 1969 near Escondido, California, a woman drove a friend home. As she started back home, a heavy fog set in. She became lost and turned onto the wrong road. Confused she went off the shoulder of the road and her car rolled one hundred feet down a slope, stopping in thick brush.

The woman was unable to open the doors because the brush held them shut. The top of her car was torn open but because she had arthritis of the spine she could not manage to climb out.

For three days she stayed in the car praying for God to send help. As she gradually grew weaker, she felt that she would not live until she was found.

A Navy officer and his family out for a drive, stopped near

the embankment to admire the view. The Navy officer heard the faint voice of a woman crying. Looking over the embankment he could see the car and hurried down to it.

Was the woman rescued by chance? God sent help because she prayed and asked Him to. God put it in the heart of the Navy officer and his family to drive out for a look at the forest. God caused them to stop at that particular spot.

Peter went up on the housetop to pray and as he prayed he saw heaven open in a vision. Through prayer we too can catch a vision of the work God wants us to accomplish. He has a purpose for our lives.

If we completely and truly dedicate our lives to God, we will love to talk to God in prayer. We shall be able to pray and receive whatsoever we ask, for we shall ask that God's will be done.

When we cannot feel God's presence as we pray, it is usually because of some hidden sin – some sins we are not willing to confess and ask forgiveness. If we really want to live by the law of prayer we must cast sin out of our lives.

Remember the story of the battle of the Children of Israel at Ai! There was sin in the camp. At last the sin of Achan was discovered and he was punished. Then God gave His blessings to the people.

If sin is keeping you from asking for blessings and receiving them, put yourself in the hands of God and ask for forgiveness. Ask for His presence to return into your life. Then you can win victories and defeat the enemy.

How shall we pray? How shall we know the answer to the law of prayer?

When you wake up each morning take just a moment to look at your life. Say to yourself: "I am in utter poverty today without my God."

Then ask God to fill your day with His strength and guidance. Rejoice in the fact that He has promised to answer when we call upon Him. Face the day with hope and courage in the strength of the Lord.

PRAYER

Lord, what a change within as one short hour
Spent in Thy presence will prevail to make —
What heavy burdens from our bosoms take,
What parched grounds refresh, as with a shower!
We kneel, and all around us seems to lower;
We rise, and all, the distant and the near,
Stand forth in sunny outline, brave and clear;
We kneel, how weak; we rise, how full of power!
Why, therefore, should we do ourselves this wrong?

— Richard Chenevix Trench

22

Do Something Beautiful

"But Jesus said, let her alone; why are you troubling her? She has done a good and beautiful thing to Me – praiseworthy and noble." – Mark 14:6 (From the Amplified New Testament)

Jesus could read the purpose in the woman's heart. He was grateful for the act of love and devotion which caused her to pour her expensive ointment over His head. He considered it the anointing of His body for His burying.

She did a good and a beautiful thing when she used what she had for the anointing of Christ. She showed her great love for Him in spite of opposition and criticism.

In return for the love she showed, Jesus said: "Wherever this gospel shall be preached, it shall be spoken of, for a memorial of her" (Mark 14:9).

Mary did a beautiful thing because she planned in her heart to do something sacrificial for her Christ.

Mary did a beautiful thing because she was unselfish. It was often a custom for a host to sprinkle a drop or two of sweet-smelling oil on a guest of honor. Mary used all that she had.

Mary wrought a good work because she loved greatly.

Today we do not anoint people with expensive oil, but the oil of love is never out of fashion.

The thing about Mary's gift was the lavish expensiveness of it. Some commentators say that at that time the cost of the alabaster box of ointment was equal to a man's salary for a year.

Sometimes we do a great amount of good by doing something big and beautiful. Mary's story has lived on and on, inspiring many thousands of people.

Giving to the poor and needy is worthy but it does not excuse us from showing our love for Christ in other ways also.

We ask ourselves the question, How can I do a good work?

We can start by using our time, talent, and money to serve in every way open to us.

Parents should teach their children to enjoy doing good works for others. A popular slogan for a number of years has been: Drive carefully, the life you save may be your own. The good things we do for others may reward us when we least expect it.

A story of doing a beautiful thing came out of the mountains of Colorado in the spring of 1969.

A mother and her four-year-old boy started down a canyon road. The car became disabled, and the mother and child got out and started walking to find help. As they walked along the mother slipped and fell. Her head struck a rock and she lapsed into unconsciousness. The little boy kept walking, searching for help. After walking several miles the child came to a cabin and found a man to help him.

Following the instructions of the child, the man, a Denver policeman, hurriedly found the mother.

I am certain that as that child walked alone down that lonely road he was afraid, but his mother's need spurred him on to look for help.

We must have the desire in our hearts to do a good work for others. We must not stop to think of the trouble or expense, just think of being a help.

HAPPINESS

Happiness is like a crystal,
Fair and exquisite and clear,
Broken in a million pieces,
Shattered, scattered far and near.
Now and then along life's pathway,
Lo, some shining fragments fall,
But there are so many pieces
No one ever finds them all.

You may find a bit of beauty,
Or an honest share of wealth,
While another just beside you
Gathers honor, love or health.
Vain to choose or grasp unduly,
Broken is the perfect ball;
And there are so many pieces
No one ever finds them all.

Yet the wise as on they journey
Treasure every fragment clear,
Fit them as they may together,
Imagining the perfect sphere,
Learning ever to be thankful,
Though their share of it is small;
For it has so many pieces
No one ever finds them all.

23

Castles in the Air
(Young People)

"And it shall come to pass afterward, that I shall pour out my spirit upon all flesh; and your sons and your daughters shall prophesy, your old men shall dream dreams, your young men shall see visions."
—Joel 2:28

People who do not build castles in the air are very miserable indeed.

Just today I talked to a secretary who told me she and her husband had bought a lot on a lake and are dreaming of the time when they can build a cabin there and retire.

Another friend told me she planned to travel when she could have a month's vacation each year.

Older people dream of ease and comfort. They long for a time of fewer pressures.

Younger people build castles in the air of the wonders they will accomplish in life.

Any person who is not building castles is very poor in spirit. The person with castles in the air finds the hardships of every day easier to take, the self-denials easier to bear, because always there is the dream bright and shining before them.

A wealthy woman went to her pastor to complain. She felt

God had forsaken her because her son was a failure in life. She had given him everything. Why had he failed?

"You robbed your son of the greatest incentive for success," the pastor explained to her. "He always received his slightest whim; he had nothing to strive for or dream about."

We should be sure we have high ideals and lofty ambitions as we dream of our future accomplishments.

Joseph dreamed dreams of a time when his brothers would not make fun of him, a time when they would be proud of him and glad to call him brother.

Through all the humiliation of being sold as a slave and even being in prison he kept his dreams bright before him. He prayed often and long to the God of his fathers. That God heard his prayers and made his dreams come true.

We must not be satisfied with just the common life we lead each day but must dream and work for bigger and better things. We may be too timid to tell our dreams to others, but we can always talk them over with our Heavenly Father.

As a girl in high school I dreamed of writing. I often wrote stories and passed them around for my classmates to read. Having no typewriter and no knowledge of how a manuscript should be written, I still dreamed of someday selling some of my stories.

For many years, with a family of children to care for, I had no time to write but I always built castles in the air about the time when I could write.

At last when all my children were through college and away from home my husband bought me a secondhand typewriter and I started to write.

As I sold articles to a magazine I dreamed of a book. After a few years I saw my name on a number of books. My dreams were coming true.

God gives us so many wonderful promises in the Bible on which we can build great dreams.

Mark 9:23 is a wonderful promise for dreamers. "Jesus

said unto him, If thou canst believe, all things are possible to him that believeth."

When winter is present and all seems cold and bare, we dream of spring with gay flowers and beautiful shade trees. We are sure winter will not last forever.

When it seems a long time before we can make our dreams come true we should remember there is always a time of spring.

When dreaming our dreams and seeing our visions we should remember a few rules to go by.

Will this dream make the world a better place? Am I dreaming of the good I can accomplish or am I only thinking of my own selfish interest? Are my dreams in the will of God? Am I dreaming dreams worthy of a child of God?

We should encourage people to work in order to make their dreams come true.

If one of my teachers had encouraged me I might not have been as old when my dreams came true. Instead my teachers always made me stay after school for punishment if they caught me passing around a story.

There is a castle in the air for every time and age. The problem is to keep working and striving to make those castles materialize.

> There will be other towers for thee to build;
>   There will be other steeds for thee to ride;
> There will be other legends, and all filled
>   With greater marvels and more glorified.
>
> Build on and make thy castles high and fair,
>   Rising and reaching upward to the skies;
> Listen to voices in the upper air,
>   Nor lose they simple faith in mysteries.
>
> — Longfellow

24

Transplanted Flowers
(Easter)

"If a man die, shall he live again?" – Job 14:14

Ben was an only child. His parents had been loving and generous with him all his life. They had been careful to take him to church and to teach him about God.

One day when Ben was a senior in high school his parents make a quick trip to a town about fifty miles away. Life seemed perfect for them, their son was about to graduate with honors, they were well able to send him to college. The whole world looked bright as they drove along, laughing and talking.

Suddenly a drunk driver coming onto the highway from a side road pulled out in front of them. Their lives were snuffed out as quickly as one would snuff out a candle.

When Ben was called out of class and told the news he seemed to lose all control. He said how much he hated God for letting such a terrible accident happen to the two best people in the world.

The pastor of the church tried to reason with the young man, but his bitterness knew no bounds.

After the funeral Ben refused to enter the church again. No one seemed able to get through to him.

A few friends covenanted together to pray for him. Their

prayers seemed in vain as he went away to college and seldom came back to the little town of his childhood.

Out of college Ben was called into military service. He boarded the train for a long journey to the place to which he was assigned. He had never been on a long train trip before. As the train sped over the countryside it entered a long tunnel. Ben was in total darkness as he sat staring at the blackness out the window. Suddenly it seemed to him he saw his mother and father looking at him. They were smiling and seemed happy. He thought his mother said gently, "Son we are just on the other side of the tunnel of death."

As the train emerged into the bright sunshine again, the tunnel was forgotten by most of the passengers, but Ben leaned his head back on the seat and for the first time in four years felt at peace. As soon as he reached the base he asked if he could talk to a chaplain. He told of his bitterness and of his vision. He and the chaplain prayed together and the world came alive again for Ben.

Even the disciples lost the glory of Easter because they thought the dark tunnel of death went on forever.

"For as in Adam all die, even so in Christ shall all be made alive" (I Cor. 15:22).

"I am he that liveth, and was dead; and, behold, I am alive for evermore, Amen" (Rev. 1:18).

The thought passing through our minds at the time of the loss of loved ones is always, "If a man die will he live again?"

We have the example of Christ who rose again. We have the promises of the Scriptures that men who believe on Christ will live again.

One summer a man from the North sent me a bucketful of peony roots. He had carefully placed them in soil and sent them along with my son who had been visiting him. We took pains to plant them the last of August, just as he instructed. Not a sign of life did we see until the next April. Imagine our excitement when we saw the first eyes of the peony plants showing. Soon there were leaves and long stems with buds. The roots were not dead, they were sleeping until the time of their awakening.

Easter should mean to us that Christ is risen! Our whole life should be built around that grand and glorious fact.

It is so much fun to watch for new life after a long cold winter. We look at each bud and the tiny fruit on the trees and we rejoice that spring has arrived.

Our Heavenly Father plans a greater resurrection for His transplanted flowers than the mind of man can conceive.

Because Christ is alive in our world today, we should be glad to be alive. We can be happiest if we are telling others of the great Resurrection Day to come and helping them prepare for that day.

LIVE!

Hush! For a new day is dawning;
Breathless I stand here and wait;
Such is this beautiful morning,
Viewed from my own garden gate.

Hark! It's the mockingbird singing,
Happily greeting the day,
As his glad tune he is swinging,
Bidding the world to be gay.

Look! See the sun just now peeping
Over the horizon's rim:
This is no time for dull sleeping;
Wake! And live life to its brim!

—J. T. Bolding

25

The First Peace Convention
(Christmas)

"Glory to God in the highest, and on earth peace, good will toward men." – Luke 2:14

All roads led to Bethlehem. Caesar Augustus had decreed that all men were to be taxed. Each man was to return to the city of his birth.

From the town of Bethlehem men had gone to all parts of the then-known world. Now they were slowly making their way back. Some were walking; some were riding camels and donkeys; a very few were able to ride in carts or carriages.

There was much grumbling; why should people be under the harsh rule of a Roman? But all were afraid not to obey.

Among those going to the city of David, Bethlehem, was a young man from the town of Nazareth in the country of Galilee. The trip had been hard for this young man, a carpenter by trade. With him was his young wife, Mary.

They had only one donkey and Mary rode most of the way, for she was expecting their first child almost any day.

The streets of Bethlehem were crowded; people milled about, talking and trading. Long lines waited before the tax officer to be registered.

Joseph and Mary were too tired to stop and talk until they had rested. To rest from the long journey they must have a place to stay. But all their inquiries brought the same answer – no room!

At last they were given permission to sleep in the stable. Mary sank down gratefully on the sweet-smelling hay and dozed off to sleep as she rested her tired body. She could feel the movement of her unborn child and she wondered if the child might be tired also.

After dark the town settled into quietness, for there were no street lights and most felt safer to be inside.

People were giving their opinions in the inn and other houses, opinions on the terrible conditions of the times. How much they longed for the Messiah to come and be the Prince of the Jews. As they talked, many quoted Scripture promises and prophecies concerning the One who was to come from the lineage of David. "Behold, I will send my messenger, and he shall prepare the way before me: and the Lord, whom ye seek, shall suddenly come to his temple, even the messenger of the covenant" (Mal. 3:1).

In the night Mary felt the pangs of childbirth and asked Joseph to help her. Soon her firstborn son was in her arms and she wrapped him in swaddling clothes and placed him tenderly in the manger.

When the first cry of the newborn babe was heard in heaven, an angel began the first great Peace Convention on earth.

The angel gave the first message and invitation to some lonely shepherds in the field, keeping watch over their flock.

The glory of the Lord shone round about the shepherds and they were afraid. No light such as this had ever shone on the hills of Judea before.

Then the voice of the angel spoke to them, telling them not to be afraid.

"For unto you is born this day in the city of David a Saviour, which is Christ the Lord" (Luke 2:11).

The angel told them how to find the Babe. Then suddenly the Peace Convention really started. A great host of angels appeared in the heavens and sang the greatest convention song ever heard: "Glory to God in the highest, and on earth peace, good will toward men."

We live in an age of peace marches and peace meetings, but many of them are failures. They do not sing and work for the One who came to bring true peace.

At Christmas time we especially need to think back to the first great gathering of the angels to sing and proclaim peace on earth. If we follow their instructions and seek for the Christ we will have peace in our own hearts.

VICTORY
(Romans 8:37)

You cannot solve all problems
  With which the world is fraught,
Nor can you fight all battles
  Which really should be fought.

But in the midst of struggle,
  In turmoil and in strife,
There's peace of mind, and comfort,
  When Christ controls your life.

The storm may rage about you,
  But God gives peace within;
If Christ's your Lord and Saviour,
  You cannot help but win.

— J. T. Bolding

26

Graduation
(For Closing of School)

"And who knoweth whether thou art come to the kingdom for such a time as this?" – Esther 4:14b

The question above was asked of Queen Esther. Her Uncle Mordecai, desperate because of the plight of his people, challenged Esther to attempt a rescue by placing her own life in jeopardy.

As you come to the time of graduation there are many questions facing you. The greatest and most prominent ones have to do with your future activities.

Will you be a great leader? Will you find a good, comfortable, safe job and stay there? Or will you just flit about without aim or purpose?

Whatever you plan to do, you now have the tool of education to work with. Plan to keep it sharp and ready for use.

God does not bring people into the world for useless existence. There is a purpose and plan for each young person living today. Your task is to seek that plan and follow it. There is a place for you to fill if you are willing to work for it. There are more diverse opportunities now than ever before in the history of man.

It is better to aim at an eagle soaring high than to spend

time aimlessly shooting at cans someone tosses in the air. Set your goals high and try to reach them.

Commencement! What a thrilling happy time. But it is only the beginning of greater things to come. It is like a party. The host and hostess spend much time in preparation before the actual time of the party arrives. Then at party time they are dressed in lovely clothes and go forth to greet their guests.

For such a time as this!

What does the Lord and the world want from you? Ask God to give you confidence. Ask Him to lead you, as you enter new experiences and places. If you go in the strength of the Lord you are promised victory.

Romans 8:37 reads: "Nay, in all these things we are more than conquerors through him that loved us."

It takes time and effort to make our dreams come true. The important thing is to have the dreams and keep working toward achieving them.

Wallace E. Johnson, president of Holiday Inns, is a wealthy and important man. He tells how, as a salesman, he was not making very much money. Blue and discouraged, He felt that his dreams of success in life would never come true. Then he and his wife talked over their problems and decided to take a partner into their activities. That partner was God. From then on He directed their paths.

God as a partner does not instantly make you rich and famous. You will not succeed without work. Demands for your time and your talents will be frequent. Who knows but what you are come into the world for such a time as this?

Most men are successful because they saw a need and worked out a plan to meet it. Mr. Johnson left his job as salesman to become a builder of homes, not just a house or two, but two and three thousand at a time. After this successful venture he saw the need for good, clean, safe places for families to spend the nights while traveling. Again he met a need.

Graduation (For Closing of School)

Every young person has some ability, some special gift from God. Paul, in writing to Timothy, admonished, "Stir up the gift of God which is in thee."

In 1962 a young man in the United States Navy was seriously injured in a plane crash. That young man lost both legs and suffered a broken back.

He determined not to be just a has-been, living out his life on a pension. He set his goal to return to active duty as a pilot in the Navy. It took much suffering and patience but after over two years he achieved his goal and was able to go back to duty. True, he was handicapped with artificial legs, but he succeeded.

As you go out from the beloved halls of your school you may forget rules of grammar, the intricacy of math, the dates of history; but take along a few rules for living and never forget them.

Count each day as a precious gift, not to be wasted.

Never pick for close friends those who have no goals in life and squander their time and money.

Learn to keep a smile on your face. Laugh at yourself when you make a mistake and try again.

Be the ruler of your emotions. Never let anger or discouragement rest in your mind and thoughts. Anger can kill, discouragement can cripple.

Develop good habits for the sake of health.

Love people. Never plan to succeed by stepping on others. Never let others step on you long at a time. Make a change if you cannot be happy with present conditions.

Be persistent. Success may be just around the next corner.

Take God for your silent partner. He gave you life and talent, be grateful for it.

God has given you this time, the time of your life, to use as you will. You can waste it, or use it for good, but you cannot get it back once it is gone. Whatever you choose to do with your life, ask yourself the question, Am I paying too high a price for the success or failure I am working for?

YOUR DATE WITH DESTINY

It's great to live in this grand age,
With every year a bright new page,
To do your best to earn your wage
In your date with destiny!

When hardships grim come on apace
And difficulties you must face
Just seek to live with Christian grace,
On this your date with destiny.

If you will always give your best
In your determined life-long quest
As you seek God's eternal rest
You will fulfill your destiny.

—J. T. Bolding